THE JOTTERY

THE JOTTERY

Thought Experiments for
Everyday Philosophers
and Part-Time Geniuses

ANDY SELSBERG

A PERIGEE BOOK

A PERIGEE BOOK
Published by the Penguin Group
Penguin Group (USA) LLC
375 Hudson Street, New York, New York 10014

USA · Canada · UK · Ireland · Australia · New Zealand · India · South Africa · China

penguin.com

A Penguin Random House Company

THE JOTTERY

ISBN: 978-0-399-17146-8

This book has been registered with the Library of Congress.

First edition: May 2015

PRINTED IN THE UNITED STATES OF AMERICA

10 9 8 7 6 5 4 3 2 1

welp

T he Jottery: It's where your best thinking happens. Maybe it's a coffee shop. The corner stool at your local pub. A bench on an inspiring section of sidewalk. A booth at the diner. The back of a classroom with great windows. The right seat on the right train. A drive up Sweetview Avenue. In bed just before sleep. The ledge of the mall fountain. The line at a taco stand. The waiting room at your therapist's . . .

The kind of place that makes you want to jot it all down, where you feel like you're on the verge of breakthrough thoughts.

What follows are hundreds of prompts, suggestions, commands, and questions that are built to transport you to the choicest spot at The Jottery, to incite that Great Idea Feeling wherever you are.

People often ask creative people, "Where do your ideas come from?" They wasted their question. Where ideas come from is no mystery. They come from interacting with this book!

Here are some practical ways to interact with *The Jottery*:

» For inspiration on a project: a novel, a sculpture, a business plan, a self-improvement initiative

» To fire up classrooms, in particular composition or creative writing classes

» As mind expanders at the next corporate retreat

» In place of crossword or other mind puzzles

» Over a bottle of wine on game night

» To get you and your crew out of an intellectual rut

» To fill in some of those down hours on dates

While many of the prompts here suggest specific numbers (for example, "If you had cheek pockets, what are twelve things you'd be storing in your cheeks right now?"), don't feel obligated to come up with that exact number. They're only suggestions. And you don't have to jot your answers down in pen or pencil. You can jot them down in spirit. These are supposed to be challenging. (Don't try to do them all at once.) If they were too easy, they wouldn't be exhilarating. This is like an ultramarathon of creative exercises. It's for pushing your mind places you didn't think it could go.

If you use this book properly, or even improperly, you should end up with a bunch of possibly good, potentially useful, conceivably profitable, maybe illuminating, hopefully amusing ideas. There is also a chance you'll come up with nothing, and experience a beautiful idealessness that would be the envy of Zen monks everywhere. Also a win.

Jot on.

You go ahead and open up The Jottery, a place where people hang out and jot things down. List seven ways you might make money with this business. (Note: It's not a café; you don't have a café license.)

You create something called Soul Lotion. What are the best places to rub it? (Don't limit your answer to human body parts.)

You're in charge of the Palookaville rebranding campaign. Suggest six slogans or overall directions the town image could move in.

You're told to design a bridge to nowhere. Briefly
describe possible nowheres you might build it to.

Where did the fun go? Suggest four hyper-specific places. If you do manage to track the fun down and tie it to a chair, what do you do with it?

You're commissioned to write a pilot script for a postapocalyptic sitcom. What are seven things you do to celebrate this cool new job?

List ten things other than keys that can be carried on keychains.

You design vending machines that sell things that are not objects, that cannot really be sold (for example, memories of meals, or relationships that almost happened). Like what? And for how much?

Your art teacher tells you to practice art by tracing the tracing paper itself. List eight things you could do while skipping art class.

List twelve things you can have instead of "it all."

List the top elevator tension-breakers, and the top elevator tension-makers.

Come up with eight endings to: "The problem with movies made by humans is _____."

Camouflage is usually designed to blend into city-scapes, the jungle, or the desert. Suggest six new things for camouflage to blend into (for example, drugstore self-checkout lanes, beverage aisles, *Matrix*-style programming waterfalls).

List ten departments department stores should have but don't (for example, the Gummi department, the laugh-track department).

You decide to chuck it all. What are five places you might chuck it to?

Complete this proclamation several ways: "You don't learn by going to some school, or listening to some professor, or by reading some book, or by doing some things, or listening to some people. You learn by _____."

A popular brand of gum is labeled 2.0. What features do you imagine gum might have when it's up to version 4.0? (For example, emits glowing pentagrams or other symbols of the chewer's imagining.)

What are a few things you think the next big fad *won't* be?

What are nine things you could say you were doing if accused of loitering?

You invent a company that uninvents things that currently exist. What are your top uninventions?

List twelve things you suspect the cool kids are talking about.

You are a translator, but not between languages. Well then, between what?

You're told by your barber or stylist not to invest so heavily in the story of yourself that you tell yourself and others. What are some alternative story investments?

Name three appropriate ways to honor the inventor of the armrest, and three inappropriate ways.

uuu

List ten things to mutter at the graves of your
ancestors, and ten things to scream at the sky while
standing on the graves of your ancestors.

Monasteries have raised money by brewing beer and jarring preserves to sell. What are some possible new monk revenue streams?

Your personal trainer instructs you to do fifteen dudesquats. Describe what you do.

List nine images you guess are on that undeveloped roll of mystery film. Also: What's *really* in that silo you pass on the drive to the pumpkin patch?

Your company asks you to write a baby book for humans impregnated by aliens. First, list your top alien-human baby name suggestions. Then, draft a copy of your resignation note.

List your ten favorite lies to tell when asked to describe what you're wearing.

Your peewee soccer team is down by 8 at the half. List some talking points for a halftime speech. Next week, your peewee soccer team is up by 8 at the half, but you've bet heavily against them. Now what do you tell them at halftime?

Make up three tricks casinos use to trick customers (for example, "The floor vibrates at a low frequency that can't be consciously felt but subconsciously alters the brain's gambling receptors").

What could ATMs dispense, other than money?

You're the founder of a new thought-lifestyle brand called PorchComplishments. It's based on embracing things that can be accomplished while sitting on porches. What are some examples of your favorite PorchComplishments?

Ideas for interstellar kiosks:

You are at peace. Now what?

List fourteen unexpected or artful uses for a school gym.

A colleague says, "I only feel clarity of mind while striding down long hotel hallways." Counter with your five unexpected places or activities that lead to clarity of mind.

What are some non-drug-related contact buzzes? (For example, "Being near the produce section sprinklers" or "Inhaling good shampoo on good hair.")

What are four objects one could plant flowers in that no one has thought to plant flowers in yet?

You're making a movie that takes place far in the future in a seaside tourist town on another planet. What are the most popular T-shirt slogans on the T-shirts sold on the boardwalk?

A dimple makes you reconsider your perspective on religion. How so?

What are some ways you plan on keeping yourself sane if you end up in an old folk's home? What are some ways you plan on keeping your loved ones insane?

List four things you prefer in the mist.

What are the top five things to do or think at dusk?

List three things only your goldfish know about you, or would know about you if you had goldfish. Bonus: Three things only you know about your goldfish (or would know if you had goldfish).

That plastic crown signifies you're the ruler of what?

\\\|

You spend a lot of time rehearsing short speeches
that you want to give to your boss, a partner, a former
friend, or the manager of a store you feel has wronged
you. Outline a speech to convince yourself to stop
wasting time planning so many short speeches in your
head.

If you found yourself in a joke or fable where you got unlimited wishes, what lesson or lessons would you like to end up learning?

Your goal is to attain the nickname "Hometown Fun Machine." What are six things you do, or avoid doing, to accomplish this?

You're a tour guide in the future. You tell a group, "Here is a relic from America's fun-dustrial past." What are five things you might be pointing to?

Name five things in your "stay bag."

Field Exercise: Go to a vintage store or flea market and make up stories about the sort of people who make up stories about people in old photographs.

Complete this taunt several ways: "Ha-ha! This whole time you've been staring at your phone, I've been busy _____!"

Come up with four technically honest excuses for not reading a friend's book.

Some cultures, like this one, don't believe moments can be owned. What might you do with moments instead? (For example, fling them at loved ones.)

List ten things to toast that people rarely propose toasts to (for example, "A toast to defunct appliance superstores!").

You walk past a building with turrets and fantasize about living there. What are six things you might actually do in those turrets?

You work for a poster company called Difficult Decisions. The posters *all* say "LIFE IS FULL OF DIFFICULT DECISIONS" and have pictures of different beers, or fancy cars, or babes, or hunks. Suggest more subjects for these posters.

List four non-geographical places about which you could say, "I'm here way too often."

❍◗◆◆•

You found a line of teas with no mystical powers. For the box and bag-tag copy, what are some conditions your tea doesn't ease? What states of mind or being will it not inspire?

A friend, under the influence of something, twirls and exclaims, "Argh! There's too much beauty in the world!" Propose two or three varieties of beauty that could be eliminated or diminished.

What else would be cool to put in the bedside drawer of every hotel room in the world?

You're asked to make yourself uncomfortable. What are some things you do to accomplish this?

In addition to freezing it, list five things you could theoretically do (or not do) to time.

List eleven entities it'd be hilarious but ultimately unwise to give power of attorney to.

The utility belt division you lead is designing a utility belt for the modern citizen. What thirteen gadgets do you propose it should have? (For example, potato gun, Chiclets dispenser, facial recognition software disrupter.)

How is your nightclub different enough to justify the exorbitant cover charge and drink prices? What features will your VIP room have that no existing VIP room has dared to feature?

List six things wood-grain paneling evokes, and four things it doesn't evoke but should. Alternately: What are nine things the smell of hot asphalt reminds you of, and what are four things it doesn't?

What do real trees think of cell phone towers dressed up to look like trees?

Other than restaurants, what are eight establishments that could rotate at the tops of buildings?

List six tips for the postmodern dater.

You overhear a young person leaving a movie say, "Living forever is for losers." What are some ways this affects your concession stand order?

You left more than your fishing gear at that motel.
What, exactly?

At the university, you're asked to conceive an entirely new system for admitting students—no grades, no test scores, no transcripts, no essays, no interviews. List some of your groundbreaking new criteria.

Let's say people can be transformed into neurons and travel through other people's thoughts and emotions. Your psyche becomes a popular location for these neuron tours. What do you sell in the gift shop?

Name four bullies (human, natural, or corporate) that you might miss if they were gone.

Come up with five time-capsule pranks.

What are three immaterial things you never go
anywhere without?

⚔

List six facts or factoids you'd like to be said at your funeral, but probably won't be.

You're a consultant that recommends quirks for piano teachers to have, like "get a tiny blind dog." What are some others?

It is said that one can take a vacation in a single breath. Where are some places you'd like to go on your next breathcation?

— ⚬ —

What are three pieces of life advice you could put on a clothing tag, in addition to washing instructions? Related: List six non-food items that would be cool to put on a restaurant menu (for example, souvenir lighters).

List five new shapes for vitamins.

Draft a text message to seduce an alien of
indeterminate gender/sex from an unknown planet.

All your selves—past, present, future, possible, impossible—end up meeting, naked, in a sauna. What do you all talk about? What do you pointedly not talk about? Is anyone ashamed? About what?

Suggest nine business ideas for that cursed retail space that will undoubtedly fail, but will give people brief hope.

What's a typical day for your ghost? An atypical day?
Also: Your paranormal advisor explains, "You *choose*
to be haunted." By whom or what would you like to be
haunted?

List four pain mismanagement techniques.

What are the top fifteen places you absolutely must visit *after* you die?

Complete the following several ways: "We weren't rich in money, friends, acclaim, or ideas, but we sure had lots of _____."

How would you fictionalize the details of your own life for a screenplay or novel you're working on just enough so that you couldn't sue yourself?

.

A local charity has issued its annual call for clutter. What could you contribute? (As always, think beyond the physical.)

You like to start the day with vigorous branding exercises to add mass and definition to your personal brand. Describe a few of them.

Invent five college majors that will have the best career potential in a thousand years.

Come up with six new sinister-sounding _____-industrial complexes (for example, the incense-industrial complex, the aphorism-industrial complex).

List five wordplay mints that haven't, to your knowledge, been taken (for example, consign-mints).

You're the headmaster of a snooty prep school for robots. What are the most common transgressions, and what are your preferred methods of discipline? Bonus: Describe the latest mascot controversy.

A coworker takes you to a store called Cranberry Depot. List nine other depots in the Depot District.

Suggest fifteen endings for the sentence, "This is the year I _____!"

///

You're asked to give a eulogy for "the death of the movie montage." How do you get out of it?

A search party is convened by the lake to find your lost innocence. What are seven things they find instead, things that are almost as good?

You teach a class called "Beyond Beauty." What, in fact, is beyond beauty?

List ten things to bring for watching softball, and two
things not to bring.

◊

Your clergyperson says, "Remember, it is known as *practicing* religion." Suggest eight other things that can only ever be practice, never the actual thing.

You are teaching a class that helps people understand their dreams. What are six requirements on your dream syllabus? (For example, a protractor, a hollowed-out Space Invaders video game cabinet.)

List six non-quaint things that will be quaint someday.

In addition to social, sexual, and industrial, what are five other possible types of lubricant?

Suggest ways we can save the cigar store spirit (camaraderie, wood, neat accessories) but eliminate cigars.

You create a popular self-help program that centers around "The Five Fundamental Misunderstandings." What are they?

uuu

List ten possible uses for abandoned big-box stores.

List six things that should never be given to someone without saying, "This'll do you right!" (For example, never hand someone a shoebox of old R&B cassettes and random mix tapes without saying, "This'll do you right!")

Write some slogans to encourage people to not recycle.

List six new cologne or perfume scents based on specific places or moments (for example, Overgrown Terrarium, 1987 Mall Parking Lot, or Sidewalk Outside the Liquor Store Next to the Sandwich Place).

In ten words or fewer, explain why it's useful or stupid to ask people to explain things in ten words or fewer.

List the seven things they should *really* teach in physical education classes for young people (for example, speed-texting, climbing glass buildings).

You're tasked with turning a bunch of snotty kids with powers not yet imagined into a team of superheroes. Which of their powers best serve as metaphors for troubled aspects of society and the self? (For example, "The Snot-Rocket shows how our natural destructive impulses can be harnessed for good or evil.")

List nine things usually thought of as disadvantages about which you might say, "That just makes me like it more!" (For example, "The static in the broadcast of this game just makes me like it more!")

List ten things that could be projected on ceilings, other than seascapes or the night sky.

You work for a company that specializes in countdown clocks. What are five groups you sell to once the New Year's and Doomsday markets are exhausted?

A friend quits smoking and is looking for ways to commemorate the accomplishment. Offer six suggestions.

You used to come here, to this place. Suggest five ways it has changed, and five ways you have changed.

List ten possible were-somethings, in addition to werewolves.

Suggest fresh lottery or slot machine themes (for example, Movie Remake Defender, Online Purchase Returner).

You are hired to create a work titled "Ten Ways of Looking at a Beach." Describe eight of the ten ways.

Someone accuses you of not being a "true fan." You don't disagree. What are seven arguments in support of non-true fandom?

Your new motto is "For neither profit nor glory!" So, what are you in it for?

• ▴ ● ● ●

You protest, "Actually, I do know how good I have it!"
List nine ways you know this.

You need to do something that will get you fired from your teaching job, but not put in jail. Suggest a few possibilities.

List six things to get high on other than drugs or life.

List fourteen activities about which you might yell at younger people, "Do it while you still can!"

There is an insanely long line. You say, "Lucky I have my handy-dandy _____!" (For example, "Lucky I have my handy-dandy inflatable handball court!")

What seven unhealthy habits are actually healthy, according to research you just made up?

Name ten carnival prizes where the pleasure of possessing them would match or exceed the glory of winning them.

Invent two new types of jewelry (for example, the butt lavaliere or the kneecelet).

Your company released a movie called *The Last Roadies*. It's about four roadies who get fired and try to find other jobs and eventually form a band of their own. Suggest alternate titles for foreign markets.

List twelve shocking Bloody Mary add-ins.

"You ain't got nothing on me!" you yell. List seven things they in fact do have on you.

List five reasons why dads overall are better now, and five why they were better then. Related: There is talk of a new generation of power moms. What powers do they have?

What seven spiritual awakenings are highway rest stops with fast-food restaurants conducive to?

You start a company that manufactures mottos for other companies. But you don't have a motto! Offer some possibilities.

List the arguments you don't want to ever have again.

What are you smiling about? Offer eight possibilities.

You purchase a star, but it turns out to have been a scam. What you actually bought was a quasar! What ten features do you design for your quasar's downtown? (For example, floating sidewalk, floating street performances.)

❦ ❧ • ❦

You've blown through most of your lottery winnings.
What are five things you might do with the last $850?

What are six things to which one could, but probably shouldn't, add flavor crystals? (Items don't have to be edible.)

List seven things you brought along on the camping trip that people doubted at first, but now they're glad you brought.

〇

You run a popular amusement park called the Good Luck Charm Farm. What are some of the good luck charms you've planted for people to farm?

You overhear an argument in which someone yells, "This is not about your happiness!" List ten things that you suspect it might be about.

It is decided that there will only be four places where smoking is allowed. Where should those places be?

Your committee is asked to plan a sweet sixteen party that will definitively signal the fall of Western culture. What are ten elements you'd like to bring to this party?

List seven things you could brag about that people are usually ashamed of.

You are watching the water. The person next to you says the sound of a boat horn is the most evocative, comforting, and lonely sound in the world. Name five sounds that you find even more evocative, comforting, and lonely.

𝕏

The novel is dead. Civilized political discourse is dead. Chivalry is dead. Declare three things dead that have not yet been declared dead. Bonus: Declare some things reborn that are widely thought to be dead.

It is trillions of years in the future. Time no longer exists. You and your buddies persist as postmagnetic pulses. What are some things about which you could say, "At least we can laugh about it now! Though of course laughter and now are both impossible."

Your memoir is going to be called *Yeesh*. Suggest a few subtitles.

List ten excuses that end in "of the mind." (For example, "Sorry I couldn't make it. I was stranded on a wildflower-strewn median of the mind.")

You're starting a business selling smoothies and juices. It needs a name, but Smoothie King is taken, as is the Prince of Smoothies. List your next top choices (all must contain a form of the word "smoothie").

List nine ways to complete nametags that start, "Ask me about _____!" (For example, "Ask me about my collection of vintage inkwells!")

Think up names for a cemetery for obsolete technology.

Your therapist cousin mutters, "Unhappiness could also be considered an achievement." List eight other achievements that are not normally seen as achievements.

A friend complains that the complaints he hears from friends aren't interesting anymore. Offer five complaints that will restore his faith in complaints.

What fourteen things should be in a classic junk drawer? Bonus: What should be in a postmodern, non-classic junk drawer?

◖◉●○

Your company wants to invent something called
a PervAlert. What should it do, exactly? Have three
suggestions ready for the big meeting, and two
suggestions you'd be too ashamed to share even
with yourself.

List eight things that cloud *doesn't* look like.

Suggest some entities for good to fight, other than evil.

What are some places that might be the next frontier for snooty, highbrow store clerks now that music and video stores are fading?

What nine things are *right* with high school?

List ten new types of czar (for example, Dried Fruit Czar).

A colleague has written "1,001 Uses for Human Saliva." Somehow, it is your duty to come up with uses 1,002 through 1,012.

You're in charge of coming up with potential sounds for the company's new Unconventional White Noise Machine. List them here. (For example, dog dreaming about rain, toddler learning how to snap, phone vibrating on an angel's pillow.)

You gain a new perspective. What are some things you miss about the old perspective?

List seven uses for decommissioned street mailboxes.

You open a café for all the wrong reasons. What are seven of these wrong reasons?

What are eight heretofore unimaginable toaster pastry fillings?

Invent five down-home, yet touched with the mystical, hiccup or bad breath remedies.

List ways to answer the question, "Where are you from, originally?" that don't involve cities or countries.

Just what is it about that night that compels and
haunts and drives you, all these years later?

What are four things slow ceiling fans stir up, other than air?

You decide to go to a cabin in the woods and make a list of what's truly important. List twelve inspirational amenities you've stocked this cabin with (for example, vintage phone books, high school science lab equipment, wallpaper catalogs).

A service specializes in planning vacations that seem unremarkable at the time, but that people look back on with an almost unbearable fondness and longing. Suggest a few itineraries.

What could you put in that little yard pond, other than fish?

Suggest nine fresh subjects for trading cards that could reenergize the trading card business (for example, Titans of Programming, Great Wine Choosers).

Your fortune says, "Most people are most people." You interpret this to mean what?

Your cobbler says, "Perhaps meaning resides in the act of asking where meaning resides." Counter with nine places where meaning in fact resides. (For example, "Meaning lives here, in this old TV hanging in this shoe repair shop!")

:
:
:
:

You're the president of the Payphone Preservation Society. What are the top eight things people suspect the society is a front for?

What do you guess will be the last five products to get drink holders?

You are walking through a cemetery with a friend and say, "Perhaps things are and are not as tragic as we suspect." List the top ways you'd like your grave mocked or lightheartedly desecrated.

List three things or belief systems you boast about having outgrown.

What are ten things you're not qualified to do, and proud of it?

uuu

Pinball games are usually themed around movies or evocative things like the circus and poker. Come up with some bold new pinball themes that are exciting precisely because they aren't exciting (for example, locksmith apprenticeship, cleaning the aquarium).

Picture your fantasy garden. What states of mind are blossoming there? Which ones are withering?

You keep explaining your ring means you're married not to a person or theology, but to _____.

It seems like you give the same three ideas every time you're asked to save a dying industry. What are they? Also: What do you predict will be the next industries you'll be asked to save?

You boast that you're out of the loop. What are seven loops you're currently out of?

≣

Name eleven things that could be advertised on matchbooks, beyond art schools.

You get to the ballpark early to watch batting practice, and the manager leans over the fence and says to you, "Eternity isn't as long as you think." What are five sports that don't currently exist but that people will be playing in the future?

List seven unspectacular things happening around us that if they stopped happening would seem spectacular.

While working for a cosmetics company, you create a hair gel that allows hair to be slicked into planes beyond the physical realm. What are some outlandish perks you request in your next contract?

Suggest ten possible names for your homebrew.

What would be different about a world without
advertising?

List ten symptoms of the Branch Library Blues. Related: What are seven symptoms that might lead you to say, "Looks like somebody has a case of the Thursdays!"?

You are a genius fireworks engineer. List six shapes your fireworks explode into.

You're asked to give the keynote speech at the
Toddlers' Choice Awards. What are four jokes or
references you ultimately decide are inappropriate
for the occasion?

Suggest eight places where indicator strips could be placed and what they would indicate.

The word and concept "popular" no longer exist. How does this change how people make decisions?

You lose a lot of work in an electronics mishap and need to redo it. List six ways you can make it better this time. How might you make it worse?

You've run out of things to mock and need to create your own mockables. Where do you start?

Your opponents think they're about to defeat you. You ominously announce, "You forgot about just one thing." List some things your opponents might have forgotten about.

What, other than sweeteners, could be contained in, and liberated from, packets?

When you become an adult, you put away childish things. Then, you pick a bunch of them back up again. Which ones?

List seven things that you are glad exist, but don't feel a need to own. Related: What is there about which you could say, "I don't like it, but I'm glad others do"?

—•—

What could replace bags?

Come up with ten marketing phrases that adhere to the following format: "We don't sell *thing*; we're really selling *concept*." (For example, "We don't sell tater tots; we're really selling bemusement.")

You're given unprecedented access. List ways you squander it.

You're counseling a child who missed a trip to the amusement park. You say, "I know roller coasters are fun, but do you know what else is fun?" List eight things no right-thinking child would find fun.

As you set a cup of coffee down with authority at the diner, you say, "I still believe in a well-placed headband!" List nine other "I still believe" sayings that would go well with an authoritative setting-down of a cup of diner coffee.

You walk into a lobby and, as always, are asked, "Are you here for the big meeting?" You're not. What are five ambiguous possible responses, other than no? What are five things you suspect the meeting is for?

Someone tells you veterinarians have bad taste in pizza. Counter with four more questionable occupation-based axioms.

Your street-corner college somehow gets accredited. List seven student clubs.

❦

List ten nonexistent but necessary hotlines.

91

What are twelve things you could swat away, other
than small bugs and annoying suggestions?

What are seven skills you'd consider dropping out of society for to cultivate under the tutelage of a master?

You finally quit your job and started a granola company. Come up with some next-level names for your blends, names where no granola has gone before (for example, no harvests or mountains or crunches).

◗ ◉ ● ○

You inherit a cool van with a porthole window in back. An artist offers to paint a mural on it. Suggest nine scenes (no sunsets) that would help prove van mural is a vital art form again.

Invent three mild curses to put on people that will irritate but not ruin them.

List four places where you wouldn't even have thought to cheat if there hadn't been a sign saying, "No cheating."

wm

Suggest five possibilities for a fifth playing card suit. Then, list nine new and possibly controversial icons for polo shirt chest logos.

List six ways you could be wasting time more
inefficiently.

What are four potential kinks in your master plan?

List seven depressing but appropriate conversions for a grand old bank building.

You buy something called Success in a Box, but never open it. Why not? Where do you keep the box?

What five acts of common decency will be extinct within twenty years? What will they be replaced with?

You work for a company that enables people to send emails to the past that are guaranteed never to get there. What questions are on your FAQ page?

What are seven themes for ocean cruises that people will enjoy, and enjoy making fun of?

What are the five least worthy charities?

◊

Someone gobbling samples at the cheese counter explains that French has a word meaning "spiritually aroused by very small sinks." What are some objects that spiritually arouse you, for which words probably exist in other languages?

You're in a home improvement store and a friend complains that there are no more experts. List eight types of expert that are flourishing now more than ever.

Watching a track meet, you overhear an assistant coach say, "Competition at once sharpens and dulls all that is vital." List five usually noncompetitive things that could be made competitive.

What are four ideas that are wrong but you hold dear anyway?

Come up with six sayings that adhere to the following pattern: The perfect banana is the one you're peeling; the perfect thought is the one you're thinking.

You're scrolling through an encyclopedia of failed metaphors. Explain what that's like, using failed metaphors.

— ● —

Someone assures you that whatever one worries about most almost never comes to pass. What do you start strategically worrying about?

❍◗◐◖

Come up with some new numbers.

What are four ways to show emotion toward a trophy other than hoisting or kissing it? What are three ways to withhold emotion from trophies?

What are the saddest foods to feed squirrels or birds?

"Greatness isn't as great as you think," someone great tells you. What are three ways you could prove them wrong?

III

You're in the business of turning vacant corners into old, abandoned gas stations. Suggest some slogans to appear on the dilapidated signs.

Your personal stylist says, "It is more important to wear T-shirts that express who you are *not*." Describe six shirts you'd wear to follow this advice.

You have a major awakening at a public aquarium, but by the time you leave it goes back to sleep. Where else might you go to reawaken it?

You finally get out of your own head. What are the first three places you go?

You host an Unanswerable Trivia Night. What are the six question categories? List names for your trivia team so clever they render your trivia performance immaterial.

List five things that remind you of what you love.
(Note: These should not be the actual things you love,
just the reminders.)

You've broken free of desires. Now what do you want?

You overhear a pickup artist say, "I wish I could put your body into words. But also I'm glad I can't." What do you suspect this pickup artist does for a living? What do you hope he doesn't do?

What could you walk on an "invisible dog" leash, other than invisible dogs?

What are six good mottos for a foosball team? What are some terrible mottos for a foosball team?

Make up some homework assignments for people who think they've stopped learning. Now suggest some homework assignments for people who are learning too much and need to slow down.

List the five most prestigious tote bags on the moon, in descending order of prestige.

What inspires you to say, "You realize how silly it is when you see other people do it"?

What are the main forms of transportation in the year 3000? (Note: If it is currently the year 3000, use the year 4000.)

List eight places or things people should be encouraged to surf that they are not currently encouraged to.

What are some objects or concepts that could be improved with stripes on the side?

List eight things that make you sad that aren't usually considered sad (for example, caulk guns).

List seven "million-dollar views" that are not associated with bodies of water or skylines.

Describe seven jittery images in your time-machine-traveling-through-time montage—ones that have not, to your knowledge, appeared in time machine montages before.

List at least ten groups about which you could grandly announce, "These are my people!"

◐

We find and begin trading with life on other planets. A "Buy Earth-made" campaign is started. You try, but what are seven alien products you *really* don't want to live without?

A friend tells you to spend more time basking in your own fabulousness. List six places where you might do this. Where should one never bask in one's own fabulousness?

Suggest lines for seducing Mother Nature.

You run an innovative soft-serve frozen treat shop. Not innovative so much because of the flavors, but because of the containers into which you dispense the soft-serve. Describe the containers.

Write fourteen endings to: "It's not about race or class, it's about _____."

List three holy alliances you're involved in, three unholy alliances, and one that toggles between holy and unholy.

What are the top slang terms used in Hell?

Finish this sentence five ways: "Wanting _____ does not make me a weirdo!"

What are four fads you wish you'd embraced, and four you wish you hadn't?

—•—

Apply the phrase "I guess it just wasn't meant to be" to some things that were clearly meant to be.

You say, "What am I doing up this early?" List six things you might be doing up that early.

Your barista says if you're *searching* for meaning, you're already going in the wrong direction. What, in addition to a $2 tip, might it be appropriate to leave?

You're a stowaway on a space cruiser. What are six things on your Interplanetary Void Bucket List?

What are some ways you could grift yourself and come out ahead?

Name the ten establishments that comprise the strip mall of your dreams. Bonus: List the ten establishments that are in your nemesis's dream strip mall.

List nine cool ways old portable toilets could be repurposed, after a thorough cleaning.

Make seven negative statements lessened with,
" . . . but in a good way!" (For example, "My bunion
surgery was botched . . . but in a good way!")

List six non-obvious remote control toys you'd like to possess or invent (for example, a remote-controlled twist tie or a remote-controlled miniature flea market).

"What's the point of a realistic fantasy?" asks the person across from you in the waiting room at the oil change place. Offer six suggestions.

It is said there are only five basic plots. What are five non-basic plots?

The grizzled gas station attendant says, "A lot more than fuel comes out of these old pumps." Like what, do you suspect?

List three things happening so gradually you don't even realize it, and three things happening so fast you don't even realize it.

What are six fresh uses for an abandoned skate park?

List ten unique items sold at the inconvenience store you run.

You invent a moral price checker, which automatically calculates the moral cost of various acts, and sell it at state fairs around the country. What acts do you test with the checker for the purpose of crowd demonstrations?

100

From the back booth of a steakhouse you overhear,
"All corruption is pure." What are some other dubious
but seductive steakhouse aphorisms?

List everything you love about nothingness. What do you say when you want to get nothingness out of bed the next morning?

The person next to you at a dinner party claims to be the Poet Laureate of Indoor Waterparks. Counter with five comparable poet laureateships you might hold.

List innovative cocktail ingredients (for example, a splash of reality show hot tub water).

Write four questions about the meaning of life you'd be best off asking a hardware store clerk. (For example, "Why does everything sound like it has something to do with sex?")

You're a coach. What are six possibilities for your sideline trademark? (Can be clothing, accessory, or gesture.)

Suggest ten fresh endings to "Join me or _____!"

List five things that want to be free, and five that want to be expensive.

What are eleven things you could carry around in a large musical instrument case, other than large musical instruments or guns?

What are some professional wrestling characters that have not, to your knowledge, been used yet? (For example, The Seminary Student, The '90s Slacker, The Sock Section Browser.)

List eight possible locales for a picnic area to end all picnic areas.

✕

What are six venues you'd most like to be or have
been the make-out queen or king of? (For example,
The Make-Out King of the College Town Laundromat.)

What five things that currently do not exist in collapsible form should exist in collapsible form?

Your company makes sprays that block things other than the rays of the sun. Like what?

List six searing images from history you could use on flyers promoting your upcoming DJ set.

What within ten yards of you may end up in a museum someday?

What are six bad ideas or events about which you could say, "Well, at least it's getting a conversation started"?

List eight ways to finish the statement: "Every generation gets the _____ it deserves!" Suggest seven places to yell it.

When paper newspapers go extinct, what are six things people could carry under their arms instead?

◦●◦◦

What new Halls of Fame do we need?

Finish this sentence seven ways: "In many ways, I'm still just a _____." (For example, "In many ways, I'm still just a teen interviewing for my first job at the quarry.")

What things might inspire you to say, "All is right with the world"?

Finish this statement nine ways: "These kids with their _____!"

What are two features that dictionary definitions of words should contain but currently don't? (For example, how frequently it is used as an S&M safe word.)

will

You finally become a platinum member. What perks do you expect? What perks do you refuse on the grounds that they are too ostentatious?

List eight celebrations you could or should hold on a
fire escape.

Complete this phrase six ways: "Maybe this is the _____ talking, but I really love _____!" (For example, "Maybe this is the electronic cigarette vapor talking, but I really love reusing jam jars!")

What else could we hide in lipstick tubes?

‖‖

Someone in line angrily asks, "Where do you get off?" List ten places.

List six things your X-ray vision can't penetrate. What's the thing it can penetrate, but you wish it couldn't?

The bartender laments that culturally, we're living in the past, while technologically, we're living in the future. What are five things you suspect this bartender should be doing instead of tending bar?

List nine things the journey of a thousand miles begins with, besides a single step.

ACKNOWLEDGEMENTS

Thank you, Devin McIntyre, Izzy Grinspan, Meg Leder, and Joe Selsberg.